Other Poetry Works in the Bloomsbury Series

# EMILY DICKINSON

## Selected Poems

BLOOMSBURY
POETRY
CLASSICS

St. Martin's Press
New York

EMILY DICKINSON: SELECTED POEMS. Copyright © 1992 by
Bloomsbury Publishing Ltd. All rights reserved. Printed in the United
States of America. No part of this book may be used or reproduced in
any manner whatsoever without written permission except in the case
of brief quotations embodied in critical articles or reviews. For
information, address St. Martin's Press, 175 Fifth Avenue,
New York, N.Y. 10010.

*Jacket design by Jeff Fisher*

Library of Congress Cataloging-in-Publication Data
Dickinson, Emily, 1830–1886.
[Poems. Selections]
Selected poems / Emily Dickinson.
p.     cm. — (Bloomsbury poetry classics)
ISBN 0-312-09752-2 (hardcover)
    I. Title.    II. Series.
        PS1541.A6    1993c
811'.4—dc20        93-25504        CIP

Selection by Ian Hamilton
First published in Great Britain by Bloomsbury Publishing Ltd.

First U.S. Edition: September 1993

10 9 8 7 6 5 4 3

# CONTENTS

Adrift! A little boat adrift!
And night is coming down!
Will *no* one guide a little boat
Unto the nearest town?

So Sailors say – on yesterday –
Just as the dusk was brown
One little boat gave up its strife
And gurgled down and down.

So angels say – on yesterday –
Just as the dawn was red
One little boat – o'erspent with gales –
Retrimmed its masts – redecked its sails –
And shot – exultant on!

*1896*

Nobody knows this little Rose –
It might a pilgrim be
Did I not take it from the ways
And lift it up to thee.
Only a Bee will miss it –
Only a Butterfly,
Hastening from far journey –
On its breast to lie –
Only a Bird will wonder –
Only a Breeze will sigh –
Ah Little Rose – how easy
For such as thee to die!

*1891*

Before the ice is in the pools –
Before the skaters go,
Or any cheek at nightfall
Is tarnished by the snow –

Before the fields have finished,
Before the Christmas tree,
Wonder upon wonder
Will arrive to me!

What we touch the hems of
On a summer's day –
What is only walking
Just a bridge away –

That which sings so – speaks so –
When there's no one here –
Will the frock I wept in
Answer me to wear?

1896

I never lost as much but twice,
And that was in the sod.
Twice have I stood a beggar
Before the door of God!

Angels – twice descending
Reimbursed my store –
Burglar! Banker – Father!
I am poor once more!

*1890*

Success is counted sweetest
By those who ne'er succeed.
To comprehend a nectar
Requires sorest need.

Not one of all the purple Host
Who took the Flag today
Can tell the definition
So clear of Victory

As he defeated – dying –
On whose forbidden ear
The distant strains of triumph
Burst agonized and clear!

*1878*

Exultation is the going
Of an inland soul to sea,
Past the houses – past the headlands –
Into deep Eternity –

Bred as we, among the mountains,
Can the sailor understand
The divine intoxication
Of the first league out from land?

*1890*

I never hear the word "escape"
Without a quicker blood,
A sudden expectation,
A flying attitude!

I never hear of prisons broad
By soldiers battered down,
But I tug childish at my bars
Only to fail again!

*1891*

Going to Heaven!
I don't know when –
Pray do not ask me how!
Indeed I'm too astonished
To think of answering you!
Going to Heaven!
How dim it sounds!
And yet it will be done
As sure as flocks go home at night
Unto the Shepherd's arm!

Perhaps you're going too!
Who knows?
If you should get there first
Save just a little space for me
Close to the two I lost –
The smallest "Robe" will fit me
And just a bit of "Crown" –
For you know we do not mind our dress
When we are going home –

I'm glad I don't believe it
For it would stop my breath –
And I'd like to look a little more
At such a curious Earth!
I'm glad they did believe it
Whom I have never found

Since the mighty Autumn afternoon
I left them in the ground.

*1891*

One dignity delays for all –
One mitred Afternoon –
None can avoid this purple –
None evade this Crown!

Coach, it insures, and footmen –
Chamber, and state, and throng –
Bells, also, in the village
As we ride grand along!

What dignified Attendants!
What service when we pause!
How loyally at parting
Their hundred hats they raise!

How pomp surpassing ermine
When simple You, and I,
Present our meek escutcheon
And claim the rank to die!

*1890*

The Murmur of a Bee
A Witchcraft - yieldeth me -
If any ask me why -
'Twere easier to die -
Than tell -

The Red upon the Hill
Taketh away my will -
If anybody sneer -
Take care - for God is here -
That's all.

The Breaking of the Day
Addeth to my Degree -
If any ask me how -
Artist - who drew me so -
Must tell!

*1890*

'Tis so much joy! 'Tis so much joy!
If I should fail, what poverty!
And yet, as poor as I,
Have ventured all upon a throw!
Have gained! Yes! Hesitated so –
This side the Victory!

Life is but Life! And Death, but Death!
Bliss is, but Bliss, and Breath but Breath!
And if indeed I fail,
At least, to know the worst, is sweet!
Defeat means nothing *but* Defeat,
No drearier, can befall!

And if I gain! Oh Gun at Sea!
Oh Bells, that in the Steeples be!
At first, repeat it slow!
For Heaven is a different thing,
Conjectured, and waked sudden in –
And might extinguish me!

*1890*

How many times these low feet staggered –
Only the soldered mouth can tell –
Try – can you stir the awful rivet –
Try – can you lift the hasps of steel!

Stroke the cool forehead – hot so often –
Lift – if you care – the listless hair –
Handle the adamantine fingers
Never a thimble – more – shall wear –

Buzz the dull flies – on the chamber window –
Brave – shines the sun through the freckled pane –
Fearless – the cobweb swings from the ceiling –
Indolent Housewife – in Daisies – lain!

*1890*

Safe in their Alabaster Chambers –
Untouched by Morning –
And untouched by Noon –
Lie the meek members of the Resurrection –
Rafter of Satin – and Roof of Stone!

Grand go the Years – in the Crescent – above them –
Worlds scoop their Arcs –
And Firmaments – row –
Diadems – drop – and Doges – surrender –
Soundless as dots – on a Disc of Snow –

*1890*

I like a look of Agony,
Because I know it's true –
Men do not sham Convulsion,
Nor simulate, a Throe –

The Eyes glaze once – and that is Death –
Impossible to feign
The Beads upon the Forehead
By homely Anguish strung.

*1890*

Wild Nights – Wild Nights!
Were I with thee
Wild Nights should be
Our luxury!

Futile – the Winds –
To a Heart in port –
Done with the Compass –
Done with the Chart!

Rowing in Eden –
Ah, the Sea!
Might I but moor – Tonight –
In Thee!

*1891*

"Hope" is the thing with feathers –
That perches in the soul –
And sings the tune without the words –
And never stops – at all –

And sweetest – in the Gale – is heard –
And sore must be the storm –
That could abash the little Bird
That kept so many warm –

I've heard it in the chillest land –
And on the strangest Sea –
Yet, never, in Extremity,
It asked a crumb – of Me.

*1891*

To die - takes just a little while -
They say it doesn't hurt -
It's only fainter - by degrees -
And then - it's out of sight -

A darker Ribbon - for a Day -
A Crape upon the Hat -
And then the pretty sunshine comes -
And helps us to forget -

The absent - mystic - creature -
That but for love of us -
Had gone to sleep - that soundest time -
Without the weariness -

*1935*

There's a certain Slant of light,
Winter Afternoons –
That oppresses, like the Heft
Of Cathedral Tunes –

Heavenly Hurt, it gives us –
We can find no scar,
But internal difference,
Where the Meanings, are –

None may teach it – Any –
'Tis the Seal Despair –
An imperial affliction
Sent us of the Air –

When it comes, the Landscape listens –
Shadows – hold their breath –
When it goes, 'tis like the Distance
On the look of Death –

*1890*

Where Ships of Purple – gently toss –
On Seas of Daffodil –
Fantastic Sailors – mingle –
And then – the Wharf is still!

*1891*

Doubt Me! My Dim Companion!
Why, God, would be content
With but a fraction of the Life –
Poured thee, without a stint –
The whole of me – forever –
What more the Woman can,
Say quick, that I may dower thee
With last Delight I own!

It cannot be my Spirit –
For that was thine, before –
I ceded all of Dust I knew –
What Opulence the more
Had I – a freckled Maiden,
Whose farthest of Degree,
Was – that she might –
Some distant Heaven,
Dwell timidly, with thee!

Sift her, from Brow to Barefoot!
Strain till your last Surmise –
Drop, like a Tapestry, away,
Before the Fire's Eyes –
Winnow her finest fondness –
But hallow just the snow
Intact, in Everlasting flake –
Oh, Caviler, for you!

*1890*

29

I felt a Funeral, in my Brain,
And Mourners to and fro
Kept treading – treading – till it seemed
That Sense was breaking through –

And when they all were seated,
A Service, like a Drum –
Kept beating – beating – till I thought
My Mind was going numb –

And then I heard them lift a Box
And creak across my Soul
With those same Boots of Lead, again,
Then Space – began to toll,

As all the Heavens were a Bell,
And Being, but an Ear,
And I, and Silence, some strange Race
Wrecked, solitary, here –

And then a Plank in Reason, broke,
And I dropped down, and down –
And hit a World, at every plunge,
And Finished knowing – then –

*1896*

That after Horror – that 'twas *us* –
That passed the mouldering Pier –
Just as the Granite Crumb let go –
Our Savior, by a Hair –

A second more, had dropped too deep
For Fisherman to plumb –
The very profile of the Thought
Puts Recollection numb –

The possibility – to pass
Without a Moment's Bell –
Into Conjecture's presence –
Is like a Face of Steel –
That suddenly looks into ours
With a metallic grin –
The Cordiality of Death –
Who drills his Welcome in –

*1935*

I'm Nobody! Who are you?
Are you - Nobody - Too?
Then there's a pair of us?
Don't tell! they'd advertise - you know!

How dreary - to be - Somebody!
How public - like a Frog -
To tell one's name - the livelong June -
To an admiring Bog!

*1891*

I know some lonely Houses off the Road
A Robber'd like the look of –
Wooden barred,
And Windows hanging low,
Inviting to –
A Portico,
Where two could creep –
One – hand the Tools –
The other peep –
To make sure All's Asleep –
Old fashioned eyes –
Not easy to surprise!

How orderly the Kitchen'd look, by night,
With just a Clock –
But they could gag the Tick –
And Mice won't bark –
And so the Walls – don't tell –
None – will –

A pair of Spectacles ajar just stir –
An Almanac's aware –
Was it the Mat – winked,
Or a Nervous Star?
The Moon – slides down the stair,
To see who's there!

There's plunder – where –
Tankard, or Spoon –
Earring – or Stone –
A Watch – Some Ancient Brooch
To match the Grandmama –
Staid sleeping – there –

Dry  – rattles – too
Stealth's – slow –
The Sun has got as far
As the third Sycamore –
Screams Chanticleer
"Who's there"?

And Echoes – Trains away,
Sneer – "Where"!
While the old Couple, just astir,
Fancy the Sunrise – left the door ajar!

*1890*

I got so I could take his name –
Without – Tremendous gain –
That Stop-sensation – on my Soul –
And Thunder – in the Room –

I got so I could walk across
That Angle in the floor,
Where he turned so, and I turned – how –
And all our Sinew tore –

I got so I could stir the Box –
In which his letters grew
Without that forcing, in my breath –
As Staples – driven through –

Could dimly recollect a Grace –
I think, they call it "God" –
Renowned to ease Extremity –
When Formula, had failed –

And shape my Hands –
Petition's way,
Tho' ignorant of a word
That Ordination – utters –

My Business, with the Cloud,
If any Power behind it, be,
Not subject to Despair –

It care, in some remoter way,
For so minute affair
As Misery –
Itself, too vast, for interrupting – more –

1929

It's like the Light –
A fashionless Delight –
It's like the Bee –
A dateless – Melody –

It's like the Woods –
Private – Like the Breeze –
Phraseless – yet it stirs
The proudest Trees –

It's like the Morning –
Best – when it's done –
And the Everlasting Clocks –
Chime – Noon!

*1896*

I reason, Earth is short –
And Anguish – absolute –
And many hurt,
But, what of that?

I reason, we could die –
The best Vitality
Cannot excel Decay,
But, what of that?

I reason, that in Heaven –
Somehow, it will be even –
Some new Equation, given –
But, what of that?

*1890*

The Soul selects her own Society –
Then – shuts the Door –
To her divine Majority –
Present no more –

Unmoved – she notes the Chariots – pausing –
At her low Gate –
Unmoved – an Emperor be kneeling
Upon her Mat –

I've known her – from an ample nation –
Choose One –
Then – close the Valves of her attention –
Like Stone –

*1890*

He fumbles at your Soul
As Players at the Keys
Before they drop full Music on –
He stuns you by degrees –
Prepares your brittle Nature
For the Ethereal Blow
By fainter Hammers – further heard –
Then nearer – Then so slow
Your Breath has time to straighten –
Your Brain – to bubble Cool –
Deals – One – imperial – Thunderbolt –
That scalps your naked Soul –

When Winds take Forests in their Paws –
The Universe – is still –

*1896*

I'll tell you how the Sun rose –
A Ribbon at a time –
The Steeples swam in Amethyst –
The news, like Squirrels, ran –
The Hills untied their Bonnets –
The Bobolinks – begun –
Then I said softly to myself –
"That must have been the Sun"!
But how he set – I know not –
There seemed a purple stile
That little Yellow boys and girls
Were climbing all the while –
Till when they reached the other side,
A Dominie in Gray –
Put gently up the evening Bars –
And led the flock away –

*1890*

Before I got my eye put out
I liked as well to see –
As other Creatures, that have Eyes
And know no other way –

But were it told to me – Today –
That I might have the sky
For mine – I tell you that my Heart
Would split, for size of me –

The Meadows – mine –
The Mountains – mine –
All Forests – Stintless Stars –
As much of Noon as I could take
Between my finite eyes –

The Motions of the Dipping Birds –
The Morning's Amber Road –
For mine – to look at me when I liked –
The News would strike me dead –

So safer – guess – with just my soul
Upon the Window pane –
Where other Creatures put their eyes –
Incautious – of the Sun –

*1891*

A Bird came down the Walk –
He did not know I saw –
He bit an Angleworm in halves
And ate the fellow, raw,

And then he drank a Dew
From a convenient Grass –
And then hopped sidewise to the Wall
To let a Beetle pass –

He glanced with rapid eyes
That hurried all around –
They looked like frightened Beads, I thought –
He stirred his Velvet Head

Like one in danger, Cautious,
I offered him a Crumb
And he unrolled his feathers
And rowed him softer home –

Than Oars divide the Ocean,
Too silver for a seam –
Or Butterflies, off Banks of Noon
Leap, plashless as they swim.

*1891*

After great pain, a formal feeling comes –
The Nerves sit ceremonious, like Tombs –
The stiff Heart questions was it He, that bore,
And Yesterday, or Centuries before?

The Feet, mechanical, go round –
Of Ground, or Air, or Ought –
A Wooden way
Regardless grown,
A Quartz contentment, like a stone –

This is the Hour of Lead –
Remembered, if outlived,
As Freezing persons, recollect the Snow –
First – Chill – then Stupor – then the letting go –

*1929*

I dreaded that first Robin, so,
But He is mastered, now,
I'm some accustomed to Him grown,
He hurts a little, though –

I thought if I could only live
Till that first Shout got by –
Not all Pianos in the Woods
Had power to mangle me –

I dared not meet the Daffodils –
For fear their Yellow Gown
Would pierce me with a fashion
So foreign to my own –

I wished the Grass would hurry –
So – when 'twas time to see –
He'd be too tall, the tallest one
Could stretch – to look at me –

I could not bear the Bees should come,
I wished they'd stay away
In those dim countries where they go,
What word had they, for me?

They're here, though; not a creature failed –
No Blossom stayed away
In gentle deference to me –
The Queen of Calvary –

Each one salutes me, as he goes,
And I, my childish Plumes,
Lift, in bereaved acknowledgment
Of their unthinking Drums –

*1891*

From Cocoon forth a Butterfly
As Lady from her Door
Emerged – a Summer Afternoon –
Repairing Everywhere –

Without Design – that I could trace
Except to stray abroad
On Miscellaneous Enterprise
The Clovers – understood –

Her pretty Parasol be seen
Contracting in a Field
Where Men made Hay –
Then struggling hard
With an opposing Cloud –

Where Parties – Phantom as Herself –
To Nowhere – seemed to go
In purposeless Circumference –
As 'twere a Tropic Show –

And notwithstanding Bee – that worked –
And Flower – that zealous blew –
This Audience of Idleness
Disdained them, from the Sky –

Till Sundown crept – a steady Tide –
And Men that made the Hay –
And Afternoon – and Butterfly –
Extinguished – in the Sea –

*1891*

Death sets a Thing significant
The Eye had hurried by
Except a perished Creature
Entreat us tenderly

To ponder little Workmanships
In Crayon, or in Wool,
With "This was last Her fingers did" –
Industrious until –

The Thimble weighed too heavy –
The stitches stopped – themselves –
And then 'twas put among the Dust
Upon the Closet shelves –

A Book I have – a friend gave –
Whose Pencil – here and there –
Had notched the place that pleased Him –
At Rest – His fingers are –

Now – when I read – I read not –
For interrupting Tears –
Obliterate the Etchings
Too Costly for Repairs.

*1891*

There's been a Death, in the Opposite House,
As lately as Today –
I know it, by the numb look
Such Houses have – alway –

The Neighbors rustle in and out –
The Doctor – drives away –
A Window opens like a Pod –
Abrupt – mechanically –

Somebody flings a Mattress out –
The Children hurry by –
They wonder if it died – on that –
I used to – when a Boy –

The Minister – goes stiffly in –
As if the House were His –
And He owned all the Mourners – now –
And little Boys – besides –

And then the Milliner – and the Man
Of the Appalling Trade –
To take the measure of the House –

There'll be that Dark Parade –

Of Tassels – and of Coaches – soon –
It's easy as a Sign –
The Intuition of the News –
In just a Country Town –

*1896*

It's coming – the postponeless Creature –
It gains the Block – and now – it gains the Door –
Chooses its latch, from all the other fastenings –
Enters – with a "You know Me – Sir"?

Simple Salute – and certain Recognition –
Bold – were it Enemy – Brief – were it friend –
Dresses each House in Crape, and Icicle –
And carries one – out of it – to God –

1929

Did Our Best Moment last –
'Twould supersede the Heaven –
A few – and they by Risk – procure –
So this Sort – are not given –

Except as stimulants – in
Cases of Despair –
Or Stupor – The Reserve –
These Heavenly Moments are –

A Grant of the Divine –
That Certain as it Comes –
Withdraws – and leaves the dazzled Soul
In her unfurnished Rooms

*1935*

How many Flowers fail in Wood –
Or perish from the Hill –
Without the privilege to know
That they are Beautiful –

How many cast a nameless Pod
Upon the nearest Breeze –
Unconscious of the Scarlet Freight –
It bear to Other Eyes –

*1929*

It might be lonelier
Without the Loneliness –
I'm so accustomed to my Fate –
Perhaps the Other – Peace –

Would interrupt the Dark –
And crowd the little Room –
Too scant – by Cubits – to contain
The Sacrament – of Him –

I am not used to Hope –
It might intrude upon –
Its sweet parade – blaspheme the place –
Ordained to Suffering –

It might be easier
To fail – with Land in Sight –
Than gain – My Blue Peninsula –
To perish – of Delight –

*1935*

A Murmur in the Trees – to note –
Not loud enough – for Wind –
A Star – not far enough to seek –
Nor near enough – to find –

A long – long Yellow – on the Lawn –
A Hubbub – as of feet –
Not audible – as Ours – to Us –
But dapperer – More Sweet –

A Hurrying Home of little Men
To Houses unperceived –
All this – and more – if I should tell –
Would never be believed –

Of Robins in the Trundle bed
How many I espy
Whose Nightgowns could not hide the Wings –
Although I heard them try –

But then I promised ne'er to tell –
How could I break My Word?
So go your Way – and I'll go Mine –
No fear you'll miss the Road.

1896

We grow accustomed to the Dark –
When Light is put away –
As when the Neighbor holds the Lamp
To witness her Goodbye –

A Moment – We uncertain step
For newness of the night –
Then – fit our Vision to the Dark –
And meet the Road – erect –

And so of larger – Darknesses –
Those Evenings of the Brain –
When not a Moon disclose a sign –
Or Star – come out – within –

The Bravest – grope a little –
And sometimes hit a Tree
Directly in the Forehead –
But as they learn to see –

Either the Darkness alters –
Or something in the sight
Adjusts itself to Midnight –
And Life steps almost straight.

*1935*

A Charm invests a face
Imperfectly beheld –
The Lady dare not lift her Veil
For fear it be dispelled –

But peers beyond her mesh –
And wishes – and denies –
Lest Interview – annul a want
That Image – satisfies –

*1891*

Much Madness is divinest Sense –
To a discerning Eye –
Much Sense – the starkest Madness –
'Tis the Majority
In this, as All, prevail –
Assent – and you are sane –
Demur – you're straightway dangerous –
And handled with a Chain –

*1890*

The Wind – tapped like a tired Man –
And like a Host – "Come in"
I boldly answered – entered then
My Residence within

A Rapid – footless Guest –
To offer whom a Chair
Were as impossible as hand
A Sofa to the Air –

No Bone had He to bind Him –
His Speech was like the Push
Of numerous Humming Birds at once
From a superior Bush –

His Countenance – a Billow –
His Fingers, as He passed
Let go a music – as of tunes
Blown tremulous in Glass –

He visited – still flitting –
Then like a timid Man
Again, He tapped – 'twas flurriedly –
And I became alone –

*1891*

This is my letter to the World
That never wrote to Me –
The simple News that Nature told –
With tender Majesty

Her Message is committed
To Hands I cannot see –
For love of Her – Sweet – countrymen –
Judge tenderly – of Me

*1890*

I died for Beauty – but was scarce
Adjusted in the Tomb
When One who died for Truth, was lain
In an adjoining Room –

He questioned softly "Why I failed"?
"For Beauty", I replied –
"And I – for Truth – Themself are One –
We Brethren, are", He said –

And so, as Kinsmen, met a Night –
We talked between the Rooms –
Until the Moss had reached our lips –
And covered up – our names –

*1890*

Dreams – are well – but Waking's better,
If One wake at Morn –
If One wake at Midnight – better –
Dreaming – of the Dawn –

Sweeter – the Surmising Robins –
Never gladdened Tree –
Than a Solid Dawn – confronting –
Leading to no Day –

*1935*

A Wife – at Daybreak I shall be –
Sunrise – Hast thou a Flag for me?
At Midnight, I am but a Maid,
How short it takes to make a Bride –
Then – Midnight, I have passed from thee
Unto the East, and Victory –

Midnight – Good Night! I hear them call,
The Angels bustle in the Hall –
Softly my Future climbs the Stair,
I fumble at my Childhood's prayer
So soon to be a Child no more –
Eternity, I'm coming – Sir,
Savior – I've seen the face – before!

*1929*

Why make it doubt – it hurts it so –
So sick – to guess –
So strong – to know –
So brave – upon its little Bed
To tell the very last They said
Unto Itself – and smile – And shake –
For that dear – distant – dangerous – Sake –
But – the Instead – the Pinching fear
That Something – it did do – or dare –
Offend the Vision – and it flee –
And They no more remember me –
Nor ever turn to tell me why –
Oh, Master, This is Misery –

1929

I heard a Fly buzz – when I died –
The Stillness in the Room
Was like the Stillness in the Air –
Between the Heaves of Storm –

The Eyes around – had wrung them dry –
And Breaths were gathering firm
For that last Onset – when the King
Be witnessed – in the Room –

I willed my Keepsakes – Signed away
What portion of me be
Assignable – and then it was
There interposed a Fly –

With Blue – uncertain stumbling Buzz –
Between the light – and me –
And then the Windows failed – and then
I could not see to see –

*1896*

As far from pity, as complaint –
As cool to speech – as stone –
As numb to Revelation
As if my Trade were Bone –

As far from Time – as History –
As near yourself – Today –
As Children, to the Rainbow's scarf –
Or Sunset's Yellow play

To eyelids in the Sepulchre –
How dumb the Dancer lies –
While Color's Revelations break –
And blaze – the Butterflies!

*1896*

I envy Seas, whereon He rides –
I envy Spokes of Wheels
Of Chariots, that Him convey –
I envy Crooked Hills

That gaze upon His journey –
How easy All can see
What is forbidden utterly
As Heaven – unto me!

I envy Nests of Sparrows –
That dot His distant Eaves –
The wealthy Fly, upon His Pane –
The happy – happy Leaves –

That just abroad His Window
Have Summer's leave to play –
The Ear Rings of Pizarro
Could not obtain for me –

I envy Light – that wakes Him –
And Bells – that boldly ring
To tell Him it is Noon, abroad –
Myself – be Noon to Him –

Yet interdict – my Blossom –
And abrogate – my Bee –
Lest Noon in Everlasting Night –
Drop Gabriel – and Me –

*1896*

I'm ceded – I've stopped being Theirs –
The name They dropped upon my face
With water, in the country church
Is finished using, now,
And They can put it with my Dolls,
My childhood, and the string of spools,
I've finished threading – too –

Baptized, before, without the choice,
But this time, consciously, of Grace –
Unto supremest name –
Called to my Full – The Crescent dropped –
Existence's whole Arc, filled up,
With one small Diadem.

My second Rank – too small the first –
Crowned – Crowing – on my Father's breast –
A half unconscious Queen –
But this time – Adequate – Erect,
With Will to choose, or to reject,
And I choose, just a Crown –

*1890*

70

If anybody's friend be dead
It's sharpest of the theme
The thinking how they walked alive –
At such and such a time –

Their costume, of a Sunday,
Some manner of the Hair –
A prank nobody knew but them
Lost, in the Sepulchre –

How warm, they were, on such a day,
You almost feel the date –
So short way off it seems –
And now – they're Centuries from that –

How pleased they were, at what you said –
You try to touch the smile
And dip your fingers in the frost –
When was it – Can you tell –

You asked the Company to tea –
Acquaintance – just a few –
And chatted close with this Grand Thing
That don't remember you –

Past Bows, and Invitations –
Past Interview, and Vow –
Past what Ourself can estimate –
That – makes the Quick of Woe!

*1891*

It was not Death, for I stood up,
And all the Dead, lie down –
It was not Night, for all the Bells
Put out their Tongues, for Noon.

It was not Frost, for on my Flesh
I felt Siroccos – crawl –
Nor Fire – for just my Marble feet
Could keep a Chancel, cool –

And yet, it tasted, like them all,
The Figures I have seen
Set orderly, for Burial,
Reminded me, of mine –

As if my life were shaven,
And fitted to a frame,
And could not breathe without a key,
And 'twas like Midnight, some –

When everything that ticked – has stopped –
And Space stares all around –
Or Grisly frosts – first Autumn morns,
Repeal the Beating Ground –

But, most, like Chaos – Stopless – cool –
Without a Chance, or Spar –
Or even a Report of Land –
To justify – Despair.

*1891*

If you were coming in the Fall,
I'd brush the Summer by
With half a smile, and half a spurn,
As Housewives do, a Fly.

If I could see you in a year,
I'd wind the months in balls –
And put them each in separate Drawers,
For fear the numbers fuse –

If only Centuries, delayed,
I'd count them on my Hand,
Subtracting, till my fingers dropped
Into Van Dieman's Land.

If certain, when this life was out –
That yours and mine, should be
I'd toss it yonder, like a Rind,
And take Eternity –

But, now, uncertain of the length
Of this, that is between,
It goads me, like the Goblin Bee –
That will not state – its sting

*1890*

I started Early – Took my Dog –
And visited the Sea –
The Mermaids in the Basement
Came out to look at me –

And Frigates – in the Upper Floor
Extended Hempen Hands –
Presuming Me to be a Mouse –
Aground – upon the Sands –

But no Man moved Me – till the Tide
Went past my simple Shoe –
And past my Apron – and my Belt
And past my Bodice – too –

And made as He would eat me up –
As wholly as a Dew
Upon a Dandelion's Sleeve –
And then – I started – too –

And He – He followed – close behind –
I felt His Silver Heel
Upon my Ankle – Then my Shoes
Would overflow with Pearl –

Until We met the Solid Town –
No One He seemed to know –
And bowing – with a Mighty look –
At me – The Sea withdrew –

*1891*

Departed – to the Judgment –
A Mighty Afternoon –
Great Clouds – like Ushers – leaning –
Creation – looking on –

The Flesh – Surrendered – Cancelled –
The Bodiless – begun –
Two Worlds – like Audiences – disperse –
And leave the Soul – alone –

*1890*

Mine – by the Right of the White Election!
Mine – by the Royal Seal!
Mine – by the Sign in the Scarlet prison –
Bars – cannot conceal!

Mine – here – in Vision – and in Veto!
Mine – by the Grave's Repeal –
Titled – Confirmed –
Delirious Charter!
Mine – long as Ages steal!

*1890*

The Heart asks Pleasure – first –
And then – Excuse from Pain –
And then – those little Anodynes
That deaden suffering –

And then – to go to sleep –
And then – if it should be
The will of its Inquisitor
The privilege to die –

*1890*

I fear a Man of frugal Speech –
I fear a Silent Man –
Haranguer – I can overtake –
Or Babbler – entertain –

But He who weigheth – While the Rest –
Expend their furthest pound –
Of this Man – I am wary –
I fear that He is Grand –

1929

I measure every Grief I meet
With narrow, probing, Eyes –
I wonder if It weighs like Mine –
Or has an Easier size.

I wonder if They bore it long –
Or did it just begin –
I could not tell the Date of Mine –
It feels so old a pain –

I wonder if it hurts to live –
And if They have to try –
And whether – could They choose between –
It would not be – to die –

I note that Some – gone patient long –
At length, renew their smile –
An imitation of a Light
That has so little Oil –

I wonder if when Years have piled –
Some Thousands – on the Harm –
That hurt them early – such a lapse
Could give them any Balm –

Or would they go on aching still
Through Centuries of Nerve –
Enlightened to a larger Pain –
In Contrast with the Love –

The Grieved – are many – I am told –
There is the various Cause –
Death – is but one – and comes but once –
And only nails the eyes –

There's Grief of Want – and Grief of Gold –
A sort they call "Despair" –
There's Banishment from native Eyes –
In sight of Native Air –

And though I may not guess the kind –
Correctly – yet to me
A piercing Comfort it affords
In passing Calvary –

To note the fashions – of the Cross –
And how they're mostly worn –
Still fascinated to presume
That Some – are like My Own –

*1896*

I reckon – when I count at all –
First – Poets – Then the Sun –
Then Summer – Then the Heaven of God –
And then – the List is done –

But, looking back – the First so seems
To Comprehend the Whole –
The Others look a needless Show –
So I write – Poets – All –

Their Summer – lasts a Solid Year –
They can afford a Sun
The East – would deem extravagant –
And if the Further Heaven –

Be Beautiful as they prepare
For Those who worship Them –
It is too difficult a Grace –
To justify the Dream –

*1929*

My first well Day – since many ill –
I asked to go abroad,
And take the Sunshine in my hands,
And see the things in Pod –

A'blossom just when I went in
To take my Chance with pain –
Uncertain if myself, or He,
Should prove the strongest One.

The Summer deepened, while we strove –
She put some flowers away –
And Redder cheeked Ones – in their stead –
A fond – illusive way –

To cheat Herself, it seemed she tried –
As if before a child
To fade – Tomorrow – Rainbows held
The Sepulchre, could hide.

She dealt a fashion to the Nut –
She tied the Hoods to Seeds –
She dropped bright scraps of Tint, about –
And left Brazilian Threads

On every shoulder that she met –
Then both her Hands of Haze
Put up – to hide her parting Grace
From our unfitted eyes.

My loss, by sickness – Was it Loss?
Or that Ethereal Gain
One earns by measuring the Grave –
Then – measuring the Sun –

*1935*

"Heaven" has different Signs – to me –
Sometimes, I think that Noon
Is but a symbol of the Place –
And when again, at Dawn,

A mighty look runs round the World
And settles in the Hills –
An Awe if it should be like that
Upon the Ignorance steals –

The Orchard, when the Sun is on –
The Triumph of the Birds
When they together Victory make –
Some Carnivals of Clouds –

The Rapture of a finished Day –
Returning to the West –
All these – remind us of the place
That Men call "Paradise" –

Itself be fairer – we suppose –
But how Ourself, shall be
Adorned, for a Superior Grace –
Not yet, our eyes can see –

*1929*

I prayed, at first, a little Girl,
Because they told me to –
But stopped, when qualified to guess
How prayer would feel – to me –

If I believed God looked around,
Each time my Childish eye
Fixed full, and steady, on his own
In Childish honesty –

And told him what I'd like, today,
And parts of his far plan
That baffled me –
The mingled side
Of his Divinity –

And often since, in Danger,
I count the force 'twould be
To have a God so strong as that
To hold my life for me

Till I could take the Balance
That tips so frequent, now,
It takes me all the while to poise –
And then – it doesn't stay –

1929

If I may have it, when it's dead,
I'll be contented – so –
If just as soon as Breath is out
It shall belong to me –

Until they lock it in the Grave,
'Tis Bliss I cannot weigh –
For tho' they lock Thee in the Grave,
Myself – can own the key –

Think of it Lover! I and Thee
Permitted – face to face to be –
After a Life – a Death – We'll say –
For Death was That –
And this – is Thee –

I'll tell Thee All – how Bald it grew –
How Midnight felt, at first – to me –
How all the Clocks stopped in the World –
And Sunshine pinched me – 'Twas so cold –

Then how the Grief got sleepy – some –
As if my Soul were deaf and dumb –
Just making signs – across – to Thee –
That this way – thou could'st notice me –

I'll tell you how I tried to keep
A smile, to show you, when this Deep
All Waded - We look back for Play,
At those Old Times - in Calvary.

Forgive me, if the Grave come slow -
For Coveting to look at Thee -
Forgive me, if to stroke thy frost
Outvisions Paradise!

1896

I had been hungry, all the Years –
My Noon had Come – to dine –
I trembling drew the Table near –
And touched the Curious Wine –

'Twas this on Tables I had seen –
When turning, hungry, Home
I looked in Windows, for the Wealth
I could not hope – for Mine –

I did not know the ample Bread –
'Twas so unlike the Crumb
The Birds and I, had often shared
In Nature's – Dining Room –

The Plenty hurt me – 'twas so new –
Myself felt ill – and odd –
As Berry – of a Mountain Bush –
Transplanted – to the Road –

Nor was I hungry – so I found
That Hunger – was a way
Of Persons outside Windows –
The Entering – takes away –

*1891*

I like to see it lap the Miles –
And lick the Valleys up –
And stop to feed itself at Tanks –
And then – prodigious step

Around a Pile of Mountains –
And supercilious peer
In Shanties – by the sides of Roads –
And then a Quarry pare

To fit its Ribs
And crawl between
Complaining all the while
In horrid – hooting stanza –
Then chase itself down Hill –

And neigh like Boanerges –
Then – punctual as a Star
Stop – docile and omnipotent
At its own stable door –

*1891*

Empty my Heart, of Thee –
Its single Artery –
Begin, and leave Thee out –
Simply Extinction's Date –

Much Billow hath the Sea –
One Baltic – They –
Subtract Thyself, in play,
And not enough of me
Is left – to put away –
"Myself" meant Thee –

Erase the Root – no Tree –
Thee – then – no me –
The Heavens stripped –
Eternity's vast pocket, picked –

1929

There is a pain – so utter –
It swallows substance up –
Then covers the Abyss with Trance –
So Memory can step
Around – across – upon it –
As one within a Swoon –
Goes safely – where an open eye –
Would drop Him – Bone by Bone.

*1929*

The Way I read a Letter's – this –
'Tis first – I lock the Door –
And push it with my fingers – next –
For transport it be sure –

And then I go the furthest off
To counteract a knock –
Then draw my little Letter forth
And slowly pick the lock –

Then – glancing narrow, at the Wall –
And narrow at the floor
For firm Conviction of a Mouse
Not exorcised before –

Peruse how infinite I am
To no one that You – know –
And sigh for lack of Heaven – but not
The Heaven God bestow –

1891

I cannot live with You –
It would be Life –
And Life is over there –
Behind the Shelf

The Sexton keeps the Key to –
Putting up
Our Life – His Porcelain –
Like a Cup –

Discarded of the Housewife –
Quaint – or Broke –
A newer Sevres pleases –
Old Ones crack –

I could not die – with You –
For One must wait
To shut the Other's Gaze down –
You – could not –

And I – Could I stand by
And see You – freeze –
Without my Right of Frost –
Death's privilege?

Nor could I rise – with You –
Because Your Face
Would put out Jesus' –
That New Grace

Glow plain – and foreign
On my homesick Eye –
Except that You than He
Shone closer by –

They'd judge Us – How –
For You – served Heaven – You know,
Or sought to –
I could not –

Because You saturated Sight –
And I had no more Eyes
For sordid excellence
As Paradise

And were You lost, I would be –
Though My Name
Rang loudest
On the Heavenly fame –

And were You – saved –
And I – condemned to be
Where You were not –
That self – were Hell to Me –

So We must meet apart –
You there – I – here –
With just the Door ajar
That Oceans are – and Prayer –
And that White Sustenance –
Despair –

1890

I think to Live – may be a Bliss
To those who dare to try –
Beyond my limit to conceive –
My lip – to testify –

I think the Heart I former wore
Could widen – till to me
The Other, like the little Bank
Appear – unto the Sea –

I think the Days – could every one
In Ordination stand –
And Majesty – be easier –
Than an inferior kind –

No numb alarm – lest Difference come –
No Goblin – on the Bloom –
No start in Apprehension's Ear,
No Bankruptcy – no Doom –

But Certainties of Sun –
Midsummer – in the Mind –
A steadfast South – upon the Soul –
Her Polar time – behind –

The Vision – pondered long –
So plausible becomes
That I esteem the fiction – real –
The Real – fictitious seems –

How bountiful the Dream –
What Plenty – it would be –
Had all my Life but been Mistake
Just rectified – in Thee

*1935*

Pain – has an Element of Blank –
It cannot recollect
When it begun – or if there were
A time when it was not –

It has no Future – but itself –
Its Infinite contain
Its Past – enlightened to perceive
New Periods – of Pain.

*1890*

The name – of it – is "Autumn" –
The hue – of it – is Blood –
An Artery – upon the Hill –
A Vein – along the Road –

Great Globules – in the Alleys –
And Oh, the Shower of Stain –
When Winds – upset the Basin –
And spill the Scarlet Rain –

It sprinkles Bonnets – far below –
It gathers ruddy Pools –
Then – eddies like a Rose – away –
Upon Vermilion Wheels –

*1892*

I dwell in Possibility –
A fairer House than Prose –
More numerous of Windows –
Superior – for Doors –

Of Chambers as the Cedars –
Impregnable of Eye –
And for an Everlasting Roof
The Gambrels of the Sky –

Of Visitors – the fairest –
For Occupation – This –
The spreading wide my narrow Hands
To gather Paradise –

1929

'Tis good – the looking back on Grief –
To re-endure a Day –
We thought the Mighty Funeral –
Of All Conceived Joy –

To recollect how Busy Grass
Did meddle – one by one –
Till all the Grief with Summer – waved
And none could see the stone.

And though the Woe you have Today
Be larger – As the Sea
Exceeds its Unremembered Drop –
They're Water – equally –

*1935*

Could I but ride indefinite
As doth the Meadow Bee
And visit only where I liked
And No one visit me

And flirt all Day with Buttercups
And marry whom I may
And dwell a little everywhere
Or better, run away

With no Police to follow
Or chase Him if He do
Till He should jump Peninsulas
To get away from me –

I said "But just to be a Bee"
Upon a Raft of Air
And row in Nowhere all Day long
And anchor "off the Bar"

What Liberty! So Captives deem
Who tight in Dungeons are.

*1896*

I'll send the feather from my Hat!
Who knows – but at the sight of *that*
My Sovereign will relent?
As trinket – worn by faded Child –
Confronting eyes long – comforted –
Blisters the Adamant!

1894

Because I could not stop for Death –
He kindly stopped for me –
The Carriage held but just Ourselves –
And Immortality.

We slowly drove – He knew no haste
And I had put away
My labor and my leisure too,
For His Civility –

We passed the School, where Children strove
At Recess – in the Ring –
We passed the Fields of Gazing Grain –
We passed the Setting Sun –

Or rather – He passed Us –
The Dews drew quivering and chill –
For only Gossamer, my Gown –
My Tippet – only Tulle –

We paused before a House that seemed
A Swelling of the Ground –
The Roof was scarcely visible –
The Cornice – in the Ground –

Since then – 'tis Centuries – and yet
Feels shorter than the Day
I first surmised the Horses' Heads
Were toward Eternity –

*1890*

God gave a Loaf to every Bird –
But just a Crumb – to Me  –
I dare not eat it – tho' I starve –
My poignant luxury –

To own it – touch it –
Prove the feat – that made the Pellet mine –
Too happy – for my Sparrow's chance –
For Ampler Coveting –

It might be Famine – all around –
I could not miss an Ear –
Such Plenty smiles upon my Board –
My Garner shows so fair –

I wonder how the Rich – may feel –
An Indiaman – An Earl –
I deem that I – with but a Crumb –
Am Sovereign of them all –

*1891*

A Light exists in Spring
Not present on the Year
At any other period –
When March is scarcely here

A Color stands abroad
On Solitary Fields
That Science cannot overtake
But Human Nature feels.

It waits upon the Lawn,
It shows the furthest Tree
Upon the furthest Slope you know
It almost speaks to you.

Then as Horizons step
Or Noons report away
Without the Formula of sound
It passes and we stay –

A quality of loss
Affecting our Content
As Trade had suddenly encroached
Upon a Sacrament.

*1896*

Not what We did, shall be the test
When Act and Will are done
But what Our Lord infers We would
Had We diviner been –

*1929*

I stepped from Plank to Plank
A slow and cautious way
The Stars about my Head I felt
About my Feet the Sea.

I knew not but the next
Would be my final inch –
This gave me that precarious Gait
Some call Experience.

*1896*

A narrow Fellow in the Grass
Occasionally rides –
You may have met Him – did you not
His notice sudden is –

The Grass divides as with a Comb –
A spotted shaft is seen –
And then it closes at your feet
And opens further on –

He likes a Boggy Acre
A Floor too cool for Corn –
Yet when a Boy, and Barefoot –
I more than once at Noon
Have passed, I thought, a Whip lash
Unbraiding in the Sun
When stooping to secure it
It wrinkled, and was gone –

Several of Nature's People
I know, and they know me –
I feel for them a transport
Of cordiality –

But never met this Fellow
Attended, or alone
Without a tighter breathing
And Zero at the Bone –

1866

111

Title divine – is mine!
The Wife – without the Sign!
Acute Degree – conferred on me –
Empress of Calvary!
Royal – all but the Crown!
Betrothed – without the swoon
God sends us Women –
When you – hold – Garnet to Garnet –
Gold – to Gold –
Born – Bridalled – Shrouded –
In a Day –
Tri Victory
"My Husband" – women say –
Stroking the Melody –
Is *this* – the way?

*1924*

The Sky is low – the Clouds are mean.
A Travelling Flake of Snow
Across a Barn or through a Rut
Debates if it will go –

A Narrow Wind complains all Day
How some one treated him
Nature, like Us is sometimes caught
Without her Diadem.

1890

The Bustle in a House
The Morning after Death
Is solemnest of industries
Enacted upon Earth –

The Sweeping up the Heart
And putting Love away
We shall not want to use again
Until Eternity.

*1890*

The last Night that She lived
It was a Common Night
Except the Dying – this to Us
Made Nature different

We noticed smallest things –
Things overlooked before
By this great light upon our Minds
Italicized – as 'twere.

As We went out and in
Between Her final Room
And Rooms where Those to be alive
Tomorrow were, a Blame

That Others could exist
While She must finish quite
A Jealousy for Her arose
So nearly infinite –

We waited while She passed –
It was a narrow time –
Too jostled were Our Souls to speak
At length the notice came.

She mentioned, and forgot –
Then lightly as a Reed
Bent to the Water, struggled scarce –
Consented, and was dead –

And We – We placed the Hair –
And drew the Head erect –
And then an awful leisure was
Belief to regulate –

*1890*

A word is dead
When it is said,
Some say.

I say it just
Begins to live
That day.

*1894*

To pile like Thunder to its close
Then crumble grand away
While Everything created hid
This – would be Poetry –

Or Love – the two coeval come –
We both and neither prove –
Experience either and consume –
For None see God and live –

*1914*

A Wind that rose
Though not a Leaf
In any Forest stirred
But with itself did cold engage
Beyond the Realm of Bird –
A Wind that woke a lone Delight
Like Separation's Swell
Restored in Arctic Confidence
To the Invisible –

*1932*

The Butterfly upon the Sky,
That doesn't know its Name
And hasn't any tax to pay
And hasn't any Home
Is just as high as you and I,
And higher, I believe,
So soar away and never sigh
And that's the way to grieve –

*1894*

As imperceptibly as Grief
The Summer lapsed away –
Too imperceptible at last
To seem like Perfidy –
A Quietness distilled
As Twilight long begun,
Or Nature spending with herself
Sequestered Afternoon –
The Dusk drew earlier in –
The Morning foreign shone –
A courteous, yet harrowing Grace,
As Guest, that would be gone –
And thus, without a Wing
Or service of a Keel
Our Summer made her light escape
Into the Beautiful.

*1891*

There came a Wind like a Bugle –
It quivered through the Grass
And a Green Chill upon the Heat
So ominous did pass
We barred the Windows and the Doors
As from an Emerald Ghost –
The Doom's electric Moccasin
That very instant passed –
On a strange Mob of panting Trees
And Fences fled away
And Rivers where the Houses ran
Those looked that lived – that Day –
The Bell within the steeple wild
The flying tidings told –
How much can come
And much can go,
And yet abide the World!

*1891*

The going from a world we know
    To one a wonder still
Is like the child's adversity
    Whose vista is a hill,

Behind the hill is sorcery
    And everything unknown,
But will the secret compensate
    For climbing it alone?

*1894*

The right to perish might be thought
An undisputed right –
Attempt it, and the Universe
Upon the opposite
Will concentrate its officers –
You cannot even die
But nature and mankind must pause
To pay you scrutiny.

*1914*

There is a solitude of space
A solitude of sea
A solitude of death, but these
Society shall be
Compared with that profounder site
That polar privacy
A soul admitted to itself –
Finite infinity.

*1914*

Drowning is not so pitiful
As the attempt to rise.
Three times, 'tis said, a sinking man
Comes up to face the skies,
And then declines forever
To that abhorred abode,
Where hope and he part company –
For he is grasped of God.
The Maker's cordial visage,
However good to see,
Is shunned, we must admit it,
Like an adversity.

1896

My life closed twice before its close –
It yet remains to see
If Immortality unveil
A third event to me

So huge, so hopeless to conceive
As these that twice befell.
Parting is all we know of heaven,
And all we need of hell.

*1896*

Fame is a bee.
    It has a song –
It has a sting –
    Ah, too, it has a wing.

*1898*